ART

Painting

Sue Nicholson

QED Publishing

First published in the UK in 2005 by
QED Publishing
A Quarto Group company
226 City Road
London EC1V 2TT

www.qed-publishing.com

A Catalogue record for this book is available from the British Library.

ISBN 1 84538 418 0

Written by Sue Nicholson
Designed by Susi Martin
Editor Paul Manning

Publisher Steve Evans
Creative Director Louise Morley
Editorial Manager Jean Coppendale

Printed and bound in China

The author and publisher would like to thank
Amy and Kane
Sarah Morley for making the models

Printed and bound in China

Note to teachers and parents

The projects in this book are aimed at children at Key Stage 1 and are presented in order of difficulty, from easy to more challenging. Each can be used as a stand-alone activity or as part of another area of study.

While the ideas in the book are offered as inspiration, children should always be encouraged to work from their own imagination and first-hand observations.

All projects in this book require adult supervision.

Sourcing ideas

★ Encourage the children to source ideas from their own experiences as well as from books, magazines, the Internet, galleries or museums.

★ Prompt them to talk about different types of art they have seen at home or on holiday.

★ Use the 'Click for Art!' boxes as a starting point for finding useful material on the Internet.*

★ Suggest that each child keeps a sketchbook of their ideas.

Evaluating work

★ Encourage the children to share their work and talk about their ideas and ways of working. What do they like best/least about it? If they did it again, what would they do differently?

★ Help the children to judge the originality of their work and to appreciate the different qualities in others' work. This will help them to value ways of working that are different from their own.

★ Encourage the children by displaying their work.

* Website information is correct at the time of going to press. However, the publishers cannot accept liability for information or links found on third-party websites.

Contents

Words in bold, **like this**, are explained in the Glossary on page 24.

Getting started

This book will show you all kinds of wonderful painting projects. Here are some of the things you will need to get started.

Top tip
Collect old jam jars to hold water to wash your brushes in.

Basic equipment
- Paper and card
- Poster, **acrylic** and **watercolour paints**
- Pencils and paintbrushes
- Safety scissors
- **PVA** glue

You will also need some extra items, which are listed separately for each project.

Use a soft pencil (marked 'B' on the side) to sketch outlines before you paint

Use a thin brush for details and a thick brush to paint large areas

Paper
Smooth **cartridge paper** is best for most paints. You can also buy special watercolour paper that does not wrinkle when wet.

Brushes
Brushes come in all shapes and sizes and can be used for different effects. Soft brushes are good to use with watercolour paints. Brushes with stiff **bristles** are better with acrylics.

Acrylic paints

Poster paints

Watercolour paints

Paints

Poster paints are good for big, bold paintings. Use them straight from the pot or mix with water to make them thinner.

Acrylic paints are thick, bright and easy to mix. Use them straight from the tube or mix with water.

Watercolour paints come in tubes or blocks. They are good for landscapes.

Mix your paints on a special **palette** or use an old white saucer or the lid of a plastic tub or carton.

Top tip
Always carry a **sketchbook** for quick on-the-spot drawings. You can turn them into finished paintings later.

Mixing colours

All the different colours you can think of are made from just three primary colours – red, yellow and blue.

Top tip

To make a colour darker, don't just add black – try a different dark colour.

To make a colour lighter, add a little white paint.

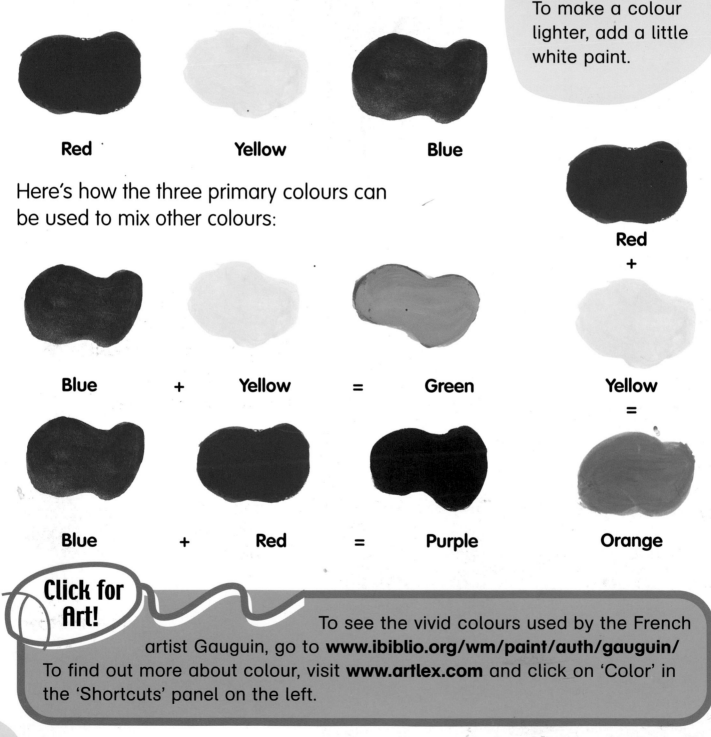

Red   **Yellow**   **Blue**

Here's how the three primary colours can be used to mix other colours:

Blue + **Yellow** = **Green**

Blue + **Red** = **Purple**

Red
+
Yellow
=
Orange

Click for Art!

To see the vivid colours used by the French artist Gauguin, go to **www.ibiblio.org/wm/paint/auth/gauguin/**
To find out more about colour, visit **www.artlex.com** and click on 'Color' in the 'Shortcuts' panel on the left.

All the colours on the facing page can be shown on a colour wheel.

Now try mixing up some colours of your own. See how colours change according to how much paint you use.

A lot of red and a little yellow gives this colour

A lot of yellow and a little red gives this colour

Fun with paint

You can paint with anything, from a twig to a toothbrush! See the box for things to try.

Paint effects

Painting tools

Try making a painting with:
★ an old toothbrush or sponge
★ scrunched-up rags or paper
★ a cotton bud
★ the edge of a piece of cardboard
★ the tip of a feather
★ a twig or flower stem
★ an old comb or plastic fork
★ your fingertips!

Flowing strokes painted with a feather tip

How many different paint effects can you make?

Try painting with different tools and materials, and test the effects on scrap paper. Label the results so you can remember which is which.

Paint effects using scrunched-up paper and fabric

Scratchy pattern made by painting with a toothbrush

Paint dabbed on with cotton wool for a soft, cloudy look

Click for Art!

To see an example of texture and movement in a painting, go to **www.moma.org** and search for 'The Starry Night' by Vincent van Gogh.

Paint effects using thick cardboard

paint dragging

To make interesting patterns and **textures**, try dragging a card comb or a twig through thick wet paint.

A comb with small pointed teeth gives a fine texture – like cloth

A twig gives a rough texture like thick grass or tangly hair

9

Splitter splatter!

Make a lively painting by spattering paint onto paper with a brush or toothbrush.

You will need:
An old toothbrush

1 Draw fish and starfish outlines on a sheet of paper. Turn the paper over and place it face-down on some newspaper.

2 Dip a toothbrush in yellow paint, then drag your finger over the bristles to spatter the paper. Try flicking yellow and orange paint with ordinary brushes, too.

3 Now flick blue and green paint on a second sheet of paper. Use different shades of blue and green to make a speckly sea background.

Top tip
Paint spattering is messy! Wear an overall, and spread out plenty of newspaper to work on.

Follow the steps above to create this speckly underwater scene

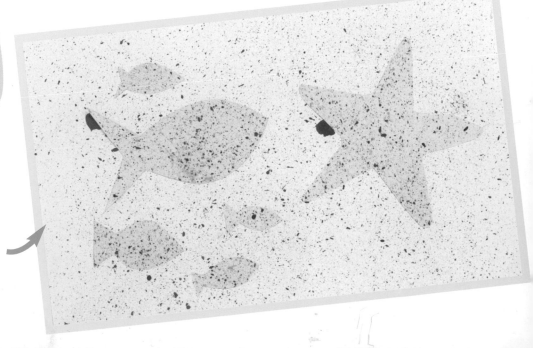

Click for Art!

To see 'drip paintings' by the American artist Jackson Pollock, go to **http://www.artlex.com/** and search for 'Action painting'.

4 When the paint is dry, turn the paper over and cut out the fish and starfish with safety scissors. Arrange them on your sea background and glue them down.

Desert landscape

1 Make card **stencils** using the shapes below.

2 Arrange the stencils on a sheet of thick cartridge paper. Use a small dab of glue to hold them in place.

3 Spatter yellow paint over the bottom part of the paper for the sand. Spatter blue paint above for the sky.

4 When the paint is dry, remove the card stencils.

Copy these shapes onto card to create the desert landscape above

Straw paintings

Blowing paint through a straw makes the paint wander in wiggly lines and creates wonderful and unusual shapes.

1 Add water to some poster or acrylic paint to make the paint runny.

2 Drip a large blob of paint onto your paper with a brush.

Top tip

To mix colours, add a second colour when the first is still wet. If you do not want your colours to mix, wait until the first colour is dry before you add another.

3 Gently blow the paint through the straw. The paint will spread across the paper in wiggly lines.

4 Add different colours one by one. (See Top tip for hints on colour mixing.)

5 Add details with a crayon or brush to complete your painting.

Sometimes a straw painting may start to look like something recognizable – such as a fluffy chick, a flower, a person's hair or an insect.

This straw painting was made into a tree by adding a trunk with a brush

This chick's legs, eyes and beak were added with pencil and orange crayon

Click for Art! To explore paintings by Jackson Pollock, Mark Rothko and Robert Rauschenberg, go to **www.sfmoma.org/anderson/** Click on 'Start project' and then on 'Explore 15 works'.

Mirror paintings

By folding a painted piece of paper, you can make pictures that are **symmetrical** (the same on both sides).

You will need:
- A large sheet of cartridge paper
- Soft pencil for sketching

1 Make a crease in your sheet of paper by folding it in half lengthways then opening it out again. Paint a band of green across the middle, just above the crease.

2 Paint in a pale blue sky. Dab the paint with cotton wool to make white patches that look like clouds.

3 While the paint is still wet, fold the paper in half and press it down.

Top tip
Try other mirror art scenes, such as the sun setting over the sea.

Click for Art!

To see an online gallery of children's art, go to **www.english.barnekunst.no/default.htm**

4 Leave the paper folded for a minute then carefully open it out.

14

Brilliant butterfly

1 Fold a piece of cartridge paper in half. On one side, paint half the body and the wings of a butterfly. Use thick paints and work quickly.

2 While the paint is still wet, fold the paper down the middle and press the white side onto the painted side.

3 Leave for a minute, then carefully peel open the paper.

5 Working quickly, paint a row of trees. Paint the trunks brown and dab on blobs of orange, red and yellow for the leaves.

6 Fold the paper as before, then open it out. You should see a paler row of trees at the bottom of the page, looking like a reflection in a river.

15

Dotty paintings

To blend colours, try using a pattern of different-coloured dots and dashes.

You will need:
A paintbrush with a fine tip

Mixing colours

1 Before you begin your picture, practise making lots of tiny dots next to each other with the tip of your brush. Try one colour first, such as red.

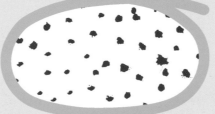

2 Now make some more red dots on a clean sheet of paper. This time, space out the dots a bit.

3 When the red paint has dried, add yellow dots in between. Stand back. What colour do the red and yellow dots look like from a distance?

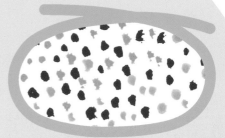

4 Now try making dots and dashes with different colours and different-sized brushes.

Pink and turquoise dashes

Dark purple and lilac dots

Blue and red blobs

Frog on a lily pad

Yellow dots highlight the frog's back

Top tip
Make darker dots and place them closer together to add detail and shading.

1 Plan your painting in your sketchbook or on a piece of scrap paper.

2 Lightly sketch the outline of your painting on a sheet of cartridge paper.

3 Colour each part of the picture with tiny dots of colour. This dotty painting has dark green for the lily pads, pale green for the frog, and yellow and dark green dots for the frog's markings.

Click for Art!
To learn how the French painter Seurat made paintings out of tiny dots, go to **www.metmuseum.org/Works_of_Art/** and search for 'Circus Sideshow'.

Wax paintings

Use paint and wax crayons to make wax **resist** paintings. The wax resists the paint so the colour of the crayons shows through.

1 Cover the bottom of your paper with white wax crayon for snow.

You will need:
- Thick paper or card
- Wax crayons
- Blue watercolour or poster paint

2 Still using wax crayons, add a snowman in the middle. Give him an orange carrot nose, two eyes, a black hat, some buttons and a stripy scarf.

3 Add lots of wax dots for falling snow.

4 Mix dark blue paint for the background. If you are using poster paint, add water to make it thinner.

Scraper effects

1 With wax crayon, create patches of bright colour on thick cartridge paper.

Top tip

If you are making a scraper picture, be sure to use thick paper or card, as ordinary paper may tear.

2 Paint three layers of black, dark blue or purple acrylic paint over the crayon.

3 When the paint is dry, scrape a picture into the paint with a knitting needle. The bright colours will show through.

Lost in space!

To make this picture, draw the rocket, planets and stars first using bright wax crayons. Then add black water-colour paint on top.

5 Brush the blue paint over your drawing. The wax crayon will resist the paint so your drawing stands out.

Water paintings

Enjoy experimenting with watercolour paints. They are great for seas and skies!

You will need:

- Watercolour paper
- Watercolour paints
- A wide brush
- A thin, pointed brush
- A sponge, tissue paper or cotton wool

3 Paint the sea using shorter brushstrokes. Use orange, yellow and blue. Let the colours run a little.

1 With a brush, paint clean water all over your sheet of watercolour paper.

2 Paint yellow stripes over the top half of your paper. Add orange stripes halfway down.

Top tip

To help the colours in the sea run together, drip a few drops of clean water over the paint.

Watery skies

For cloudy skies, paint overlapping stripes of blue watercolour paint across your paper. Before the paint dries, dab it with a clean sponge. This will leave white patches that look like clouds.

4 While the paint is still wet, dab cotton wool on the yellow sky so the patches look like pale clouds.

These clouds were made by painting stripes of blue across wet paper, then dabbing the paint with scrunched-up tissue paper

5 When the paint is dry, paint a black island and a palm tree. If you like, add a shark's fin pointing out of the water!

For a different effect, let the blue paint dry, then paint clouds in white watercolour paint

Click for Art!

To see watercolours by the English artist Turner, go to **www.j-m-w-turner.co.uk/** Click on 'Turner in Venice', scroll down, then click on small pictures.

Special effects

Make your paintings special by adding glitter or cornflour to paint, or sprinkling salt onto wet paint.

You will need:
- Glitter
- Cornflour
- Soft, wide brush
- Salt crystals

1 Wet the paper all over with a soft, wide brush.

2 While the paper is wet, drip blobs of paint in a circle and let them spread.

3 Add a tiny dot of paint for the centre of each flower. Sprinkle grains of salt over the painted petals. Watch how the salt soaks up the paint and makes dappled marks on the paper.

Flower painting

When the paint is dry, add stems for the flowers with a thin brush

Top tip

Shake off the salt when the paint has dried, or leave it on if you want more texture in your painting.

Click for Art!

For a good general children's art website including art galleries, art quizzes and information about artists and their work, visit **www.scribbleskidsart.com**

All that glitters

It's easy to make your own sparkly glitter paint. Just add glitter to acrylic or poster paint and paint it on with a brush as usual.

Adding texture

To thicken poster paint, add a few spoonfuls of cornflour. Keep mixing until you have the texture you want. Paint with a brush as usual. If you like, make patterns in the paint with a tool or card comb (see page 9).

23

Glossary

acrylic easy-to-mix paint that dries quickly and can be cleaned with soap and water

bristles fibres on the end of a paintbrush made of animal hair or nylon

cartridge paper thick, smooth paper, good for drawing and painting

palette a flat piece of wood or plastic used by artists to mix paints

PVA strong white glue that can be mixed with water; good for sticking paper and card

resist substance such as wax that protects a surface so it does not get coloured with paint or dye

sketchbook a small, easy-to-carry book for quick drawings and designs

stencil a shape cut-out of card which you can paint or print through, or around

symmetrical a shape that is the same on both sides

texture the surface or 'feel' of something – for example, fabric can be rough, soft, furry or velvety

watercolour paint paint sold in tubes or as small solid blocks

Index